Zoo
DENTISTS

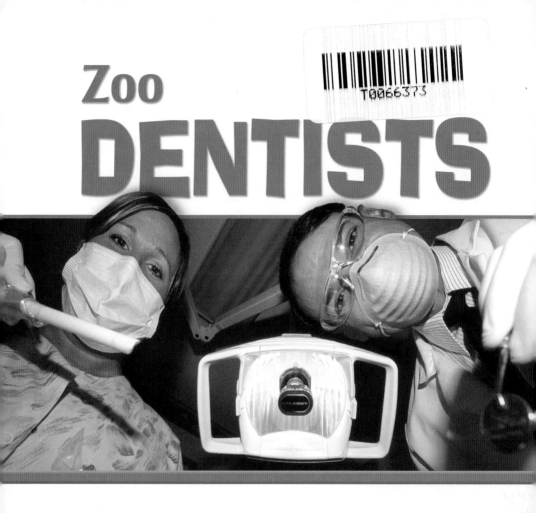

Rob Waring, *Series Editor*

HEINLE
CENGAGE Learning

Australia • Brazil • Japan • Korea • Mexico • Singapore • Spain • United Kingdom • United States

Words to Know

This story is set in the United States. It happens in the state of California, in the city of San Francisco.

San Francisco

California

CANADA

California

UNITED STATES

MEXICO

A **At the Zoo.** Here are some things you will read about in the story. Read the paragraph and label the picture with the words in **bold**.

When animals are kept in a zoo, they can sometimes develop problems with their teeth and need a **dentist**. This story is about a father and daughter dentist team, Dr. Paul Brown and Dr. Sarah de Sanz [də sænz], and how they treat these animals. First, they examine an elephant's teeth and **tusks** to be sure everything is okay. Next, they check a **sea lion**, which lives most of its life in water and eats its food whole. Finally, they help a beautiful and rare black **jaguar** with a terrible pain in its **jaw**.

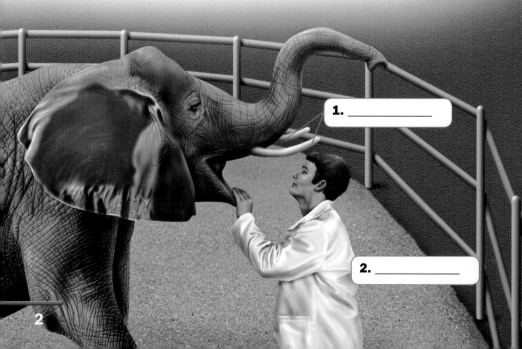

1. _____

2. _____

2

B At the Dentist.
Read the definitions. Then complete the paragraph with the correct form of the words.

checkup: a general examination by a doctor or dentist
filling: a substance used to fill a hole in a tooth
gums: the pink flesh around the teeth
patient *(noun)*: a person cared for or treated by a doctor or dentist
toothache: a pain caused by a problem with a tooth

Many people have a regular (1)_____ with the dentist every year. They hope that both their teeth and (2)_____ will be healthy. They certainly don't want to need a (3)_____ or something worse. Sometimes people wait until they experience a bad pain, or a (4)_____, before they go to their dentist's office. When that happens, the (5)_____ may need a lot of work on his or her teeth, or even an operation!

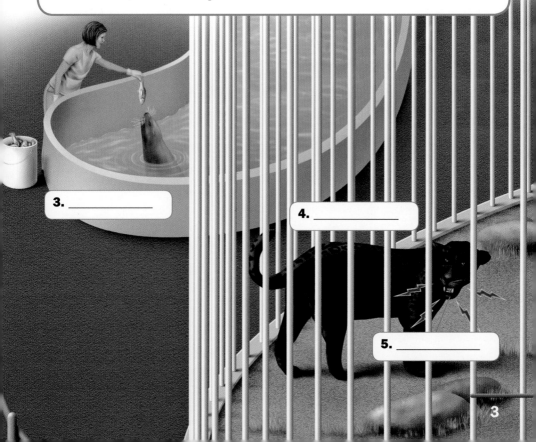

3. _____

4. _____

5. _____

When an animal has a toothache, it can't just go to the dentist's office like people do. Fortunately, there is someone who can help. Dr. Sarah de Sanz is a 'people dentist' most of the time. She most often treats human patients in her dental office in the San Francisco area. However, sometimes she must treat other patients who can't come to her office—or even fit into a dentist's chair! What kind of patients are these? They're animals! Dr. de Sanz is a part-time zoo dentist.

CD 2, Track 07

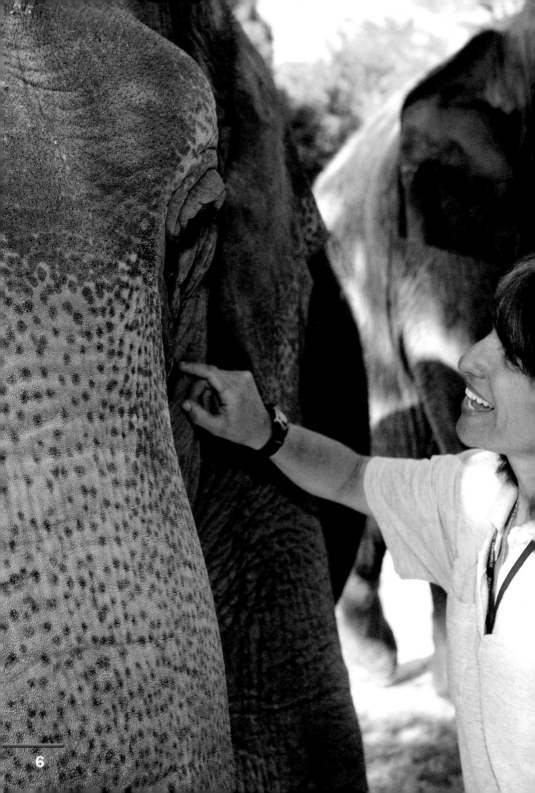

Dr. de Sanz and her father, Dr. Paul Brown, who is also a dentist, work as a team in the San Francisco area. They do checkups, fillings, and other dental work on any animal that needs them. Dr. de Sanz explains how it all started. "My dad and I started working on animals together when I was in dental school," she says. "He's great to work with, he's very **patient**,[1] and we really enjoy working together."

Dr. de Sanz's father says that he's happy that she became a dentist. "I'm thrilled that Sarah has become a dentist!" he says. But when he adds, "I didn't have anything to do with it," his daughter stops him and says with a laugh, "That's not true!" Dr. Brown then continues to talk proudly about what they do, "I'm happy. I think it's a wonderful job," he says.

---

[1] **patient (*adj.*):** able to accept discomfort, difficulties, or pain without complaining or becoming angry

Going to the dentist is frightening for a lot of people, but when a dentist is treating a zoo animal, it's not the patient who is scared. The dentist has a good reason to be frightened. Some of these patients could take his or her hand off in one bite!

Both Dr. de Sanz and Dr. Brown are used to working in some of the most dangerous jaws in the animal world. They're happy to do it, though, because the animals really need their services. Many of these animals need their teeth to build homes, catch fish, and defend themselves. In the animal world, bad teeth can make it impossible to live a normal life.

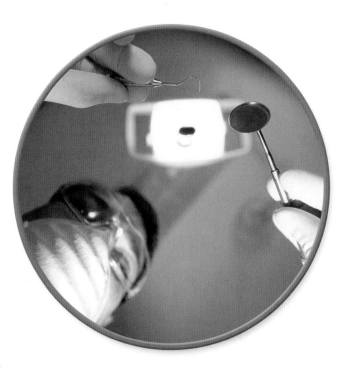

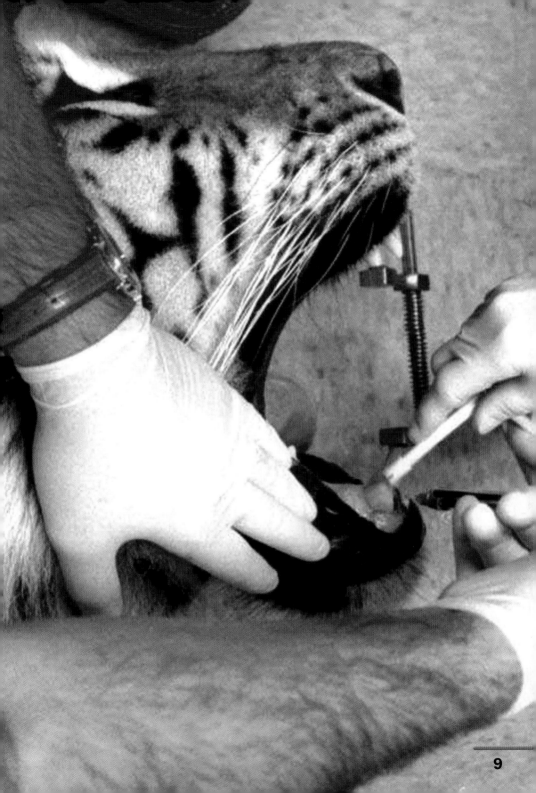

Like people, the dental problems of zoo animals can be caused by what they do—or don't—eat. A zoo employee explains, "Animals **in captivity**[2] … unfortunately they aren't **chewing**[3] on bones and **carcasses**[4] as often as they would in the wild. Therefore the natural cleaning of the teeth is not there. So dental disease is probably a little higher on the list than it would be in the wild." In addition, animals that are in captivity often live longer, which means that their teeth have to last longer too.

---

[2]**in captivity:** unable to move or act freely; kept in a limited space
[3]**chew:** move the lower jaw to break up food into smaller pieces with the teeth
[4]**carcass:** the body of a dead animal

Infer Meaning

1. What does the sentence 'So dental disease is probably a little higher on the list than it would be in the wild' mean?

2. Why do animals in captivity need a dentist?

Tooth maintenance is extremely important for both people and animals. Because of this, Dr. de Sanz and Dr. Brown regularly do checkups on zoo animals. Today, they are starting with Artie the sea lion, who is one of the dentists' best patients. "He's an excellent dental patient; he's better than most people," explains one of the zoo workers.

Dr. de Sanz talks about Artie before she examines him. "So far as we know, he is quite an old animal. He's 30 years old, which is twice their normal **life expectancy**,"[5] she says as the animal swims happily nearby. Suddenly Artie makes a very loud noise. It almost sounds like he's agreeing with her statement! Afterwards she adds with a laugh, "and he's happy about it!" Dr. de Sanz continues by talking about the treatment plan for the seal, "So we're going to just look at his teeth and see if he has any particular dental problems."

---

[5]**life expectancy:** the length of time that a living thing is likely to exist

Because of his age, the zoo dentists want to be sure that Artie doesn't have any problems with his teeth. They decide to take an **X-ray**[6] to get a better look. When it's time for them to take the X-ray, their animal patient comes agreeably out of his pool and goes to an examining table. When the zoo worker tells him to open his mouth, Artie does so with no problem. However, things after that don't go so simply. It's not easy to get an excited sea lion to stay still while an X-ray is taken of his teeth! Every time they take a shot, the sea lion moves to a different position. After a number of attempts, the dentists finally succeed in getting a clear picture.

Sea lions eat their food whole, and can eat as much as 20 **pounds**[7] of fish in one day. Even though they don't chew their food, their teeth and gums can still get diseased. For Artie, his checkup goes well and the dentists conclude that his teeth are just fine: not bad for a 30-year-old who's never brushed his teeth!

------

[6]**X-ray:** a special photograph that shows the inside of the body
[7]**pound:** 1 pound = 0.45 kilograms

Once the zoo dentists have treated the sea lion, they move on to a much bigger animal—an elephant! Dr. Brown says that elephants are his favorite animals, mainly because they have the most interesting teeth. As Dr. Brown displays one of the huge teeth, he explains: "This is an elephant **molar**.[8] They don't have any side-to-side movement; they can only **go back and forth**."[9] Elephants use six sets of teeth in a lifetime. When the last set of teeth is gone, they can no longer eat and will die.

Today the zoo dentists are treating Sue, a ten-year-old female African elephant. While they perform their examination, they not only check the teeth in Sue's mouth, but also look at her tusks. An elephant's tusks are actually teeth and must be treated and checked like them, too. For the dentists, Sue is the perfect patient because she stands quietly while they examine her. She gets an excellent report from the dentists, too. "Perfect!" says Dr. Brown, "Her teeth look wonderful!"

---

[8] **molar:** any of the large teeth at the back of the mouth
[9] **go back and forth:** move forwards and backwards between two points

So far, the zoo dentists' patients have been great, but not all animals behave so well. How much danger are the dentists actually in? Have they ever been bitten? "No, we've never been bitten, but almost," says Dr. Brown, laughing, "A couple of times we've had to move pretty quickly to get our fingers out of the way!"

The next patient on the dentists' list doesn't seem to be as lucky as Artie and Sue. The dentists have received a call from the San Francisco Zoo. The zoo's rare black jaguar, Sandy, has a terrible toothache and may need **surgery**[10] to fix it. A zoo employee explains that the jaguar has to be asleep before the dentists can look inside its mouth. "Unfortunately we just can't walk up to her and say 'Can I look in your mouth?'" he points out, "You may lose a few fingers in the process, as well as maybe your head!" He then adds, "So therefore this animal has to be **anesthetized**[11] in order for us to look at it."

---

[10]**surgery:** the medical practice of treating injuries and disease by operating on the body

[11]**anesthetize:** give a substance, called an anesthetic, to stop a patient from feeling pain

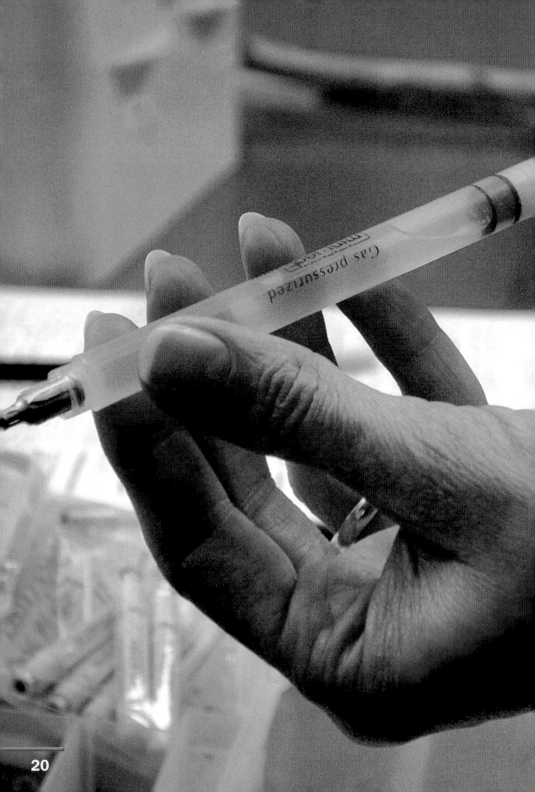

Putting an animal to sleep is always risky business, especially for an older cat like Sandy. She's 21 years old, and the drug used to anesthetize her can cause major problems. If they use too little, she could wake up and bite the dentists. If they use too much, Sandy could die. Everybody is worried about the risk as they prepare for the surgery.

First, they carefully prepare the drug and shoot it into Sandy. Then, the team moves her quickly to the operating room and tries to proceed with the surgery. But suddenly there's a problem—Sandy has stopped breathing! The zoo doctors give her **oxygen**.[12] It helps a little, but it doesn't do enough. Sandy is taking only one breath per minute! Time is running out, and the team has to act quickly. Finally, they decide to give Sandy a special medicine to make her start breathing faster. The question is: will it work?

———————————————————

[12] **oxygen:** a substance that all humans and animals need to live; O_2

The medicine works! Sandy finally begins breathing on her own again. At last everyone can start the real job: fixing Sandy's teeth before she wakes up. Things go smoothly for a time, but then the dentist team makes an unfortunate discovery: Sandy's teeth are worse than they expected. She needs not one, but two **root canals**[13]— and a filling! Dr. de Sanz and Dr. Brown must now work carefully and quickly to take out the **nerve**[14] of each bad tooth and then put fillings in the holes that are left.

Finally, after a lot of hard work—and risk—the surgery is over. The dentists have done their job well and Sandy's visit with the dentist is a complete success. "The root canal is completed; it worked perfectly as expected," says Dr. Brown.

---

[13]**root canal:** a process where a dentist removes the blood and nerve supply from a bad tooth
[14]**nerve:** a long fiber that carries messages between the brain and other parts of the body

Sequence the Events

What is the correct order of the events? Write numbers.

_____ Sandy stops breathing.

_____ The dentists give Sandy a medicine to help her breathe.

_____ The dentists give Sandy oxygen to help her to breathe.

_____ The dentists give Sandy an anesthetic to put her to sleep.

And as for Sandy? Well, although she nearly didn't make it through the surgery, she should be fine when she wakes up. Dr. de Sanz also reports on the surgery: "It went great; she had two successful root canals and one great filling and a nice cleaning, and she's **all set**."[15]

The jaguar's visit with the dentists is over this time. Sandy will have a headache for a few days because of the surgery, but soon she'll feel well again. More importantly, from now on, she shouldn't have a toothache!

---

[15]**all set:** *(slang)* ready to go; in this sense, better

Dr. de Sanz and Dr. Brown have completed another successful animal dentistry job. For both of them, it's extremely important work. Later, Dr. de Sanz remarks that people have a responsibility towards animals in captivity, especially the animals that are kept in zoos. "I really do believe that it's our responsibility," she says, "If we're going to keep animals in captivity for everybody to look at, then we have to keep them healthy."

As the zoo dentists finish another day, they can feel satisfied because they are helping these animals to live healthy and happy lives. It's all in a day's work for these zoo dentists!

Summarize

Imagine that you are Dr. de Sanz. Tell or write the story about helping Sandy the jaguar. Include the following information.

1. How did you feel when Sandy stopped breathing?

2. What was it like when you suddenly knew that she was going to live?

SAN FRANCISCO
ZOO

After You Read

1. Dr. Sarah de Sanz _____ treats animal patients.
   A. never
   B. occasionally
   C. rarely
   D. always

2. How does Dr. Paul Brown feel about his daughter's work?
   A. patient
   B. disappointed
   C. pleased
   D. concerned

3. According to paragraph 2 on page 8, animals use their teeth for:
   A. protection
   B. hunting
   C. construction
   D. all of the above

4. Living in captivity makes animal teeth:
   A. less healthy
   B. more healthy
   C. longer
   D. cleaner

5. Why does Artie the sea lion need to see the doctors?
   A. He has a toothache.
   B. He has never been to a dentist.
   C. He needs a checkup.
   D. His gums are hurting.

6. Which of the following is NOT a good heading for page 17?
   A. Doctor Studies Unusual Molars
   B. One Lifetime, Six Sets of Teeth
   C. Elephant Tusk Has Cavity
   D. Sue Gets Good Report

7. An animal might bite the doctors during surgery if:
   A. The animal wakes up.
   B. The zoo workers don't help.
   C. The animal is sleeping.
   D. The doctors work too quickly.

8. Who does 'they' refer to in paragraph 1 on page 21?
   A. jaguars
   B. Sandy and Artie
   C. zoo workers
   D. zoo animals

9. What does the writer think about anesthetizing animals?
   A. It's convenient.
   B. It's dangerous but necessary.
   C. It's not very risky.
   D. It should be avoided.

10. What does the word 'unfortunate' mean in paragraph 1 on page 22?
    A. unwanted
    B. interesting
    C. meaningful
    D. unhappy

11. Which of the following does NOT happen during Sandy's surgery?
    A. She starts breathing faster again after a special drug.
    B. She doesn't breathe for one minute after getting oxygen.
    C. She stops breathing after being anesthetized.
    D. She gets moved to the operating room after going to sleep.

12. What's the reason for Dr. de Sanz's remark in paragraph 1 on page 26?
    A. to explain why we should not keep animals in captivity
    B. to show that she and her father have a big responsibility
    C. to show that we must take care of animals that we put in captivity
    D. to introduce the idea that zoos are very special places

QUESTIONS FOR
Dr. Mancuso
Doggie Dentist

Do I really have to clean my dog's teeth?

Yes, it's very important! In fact, it's a good idea to clean your dog's teeth every day. Dogs can get toothaches or lose a tooth if their teeth get dirty and their gums become weak. Not all dogs enjoy having their teeth cleaned. However, if you begin when the dog is young, it will get used to it and you won't likely have any trouble in the future. It's a good idea to link the cleaning with something the dog likes, such as food. Brushing before meals may be the best plan for your dog.

It's very important to clean your dog's teeth.

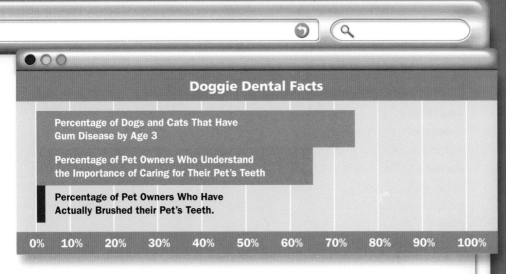

Doggie Dental Facts

Percentage of Dogs and Cats That Have
Gum Disease by Age 3

Percentage of Pet Owners Who Understand
the Importance of Caring for Their Pet's Teeth

Percentage of Pet Owners Who Have
Actually Brushed their Pet's Teeth.

| 0% | 10% | 20% | 30% | 40% | 50% | 60% | 70% | 80% | 90% | 100% |

My dog broke one of her teeth. Do I need to do anything about it?

It is fairly common for dogs to break their teeth. It can happen when the tooth gets hit by a ball or a rock; or if the dog eats something very hard. Although the animal may not appear to be in any pain, you most certainly should do something about it. If there is an opening in the tooth, it will become diseased and this disease could spread to the jaw bone. There are two things you can do. You can have the tooth repaired, which is probably the best for the dog since it needs all his teeth in order to bite properly. Or, if the tooth can't be fixed, it might have to be removed. Of course the dog is anesthetized so it doesn't feel a thing.

Do you ever fill a dog's teeth?

Yes, it has become an everyday procedure in many animal dentists' offices. The process is very similar to putting a filling in a human tooth. If we discover a hole in a tooth while doing a checkup, we immediately take an X-ray of the inside of the tooth to see how big the problem is. Next, if necessary, we remove part of the inside of the tooth. Then, the hole is filled with a mixture of silver or plastic materials. Fillings have to be especially hard in dogs' teeth because they often bite on very hard objects.

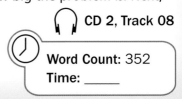

CD 2, Track 08

Word Count: 352
Time: _____

Vocabulary List

all set (25)
anesthetize (18, 21, 23)
carcass (10)
checkup (3, 7, 13, 14)
chew (10, 14)
dentist (2, 3, 4, 7, 8, 10, 11, 13, 14, 17, 18, 21, 22, 23, 25, 26)
filling (3, 7, 22, 25)
go back and forth (17)
gums (3, 14)
in captivity (10, 26)
jaguar (2, 18, 25, 27)
jaw (2, 8, 10)
life expectancy (13)
molar (17)
nerve (22)
oxygen (21, 23)
patient (*adj.*) (7)
patient (*noun*) (3, 4, 8, 13, 14, 17, 18)
pound (14)
root canal (22, 25)
sea lion (2, 13, 14, 17)
surgery (18, 21, 22, 25)
toothache (3, 4, 18, 25)
tusk (2, 17)
X-ray (14)